I0143030

SUNLIGHT, SHADOWS, AND ECHOES

Later Collected Poems 2016-2018

by David A. Folds

WingSpan Press

Copyright © 2019 by David A. Folds

All rights reserved.

No part of this book may be reproduced or transmitted in any
form or by any means, electronic or mechanical, including
photocopying, recording or by any information storage and
retrieval system, without written permission from the author,
except for the inclusion of brief quotations in review.

Published in the United States and the United Kingdom
by WingSpan Press, Livermore, CA

The WingSpan name, logo and colophon are
the trademarks of WingSpan Publishing.

ISBN 978-1-59594-636-2 (pbk.)
ISBN 978-1-59594-952-3 (ebk.)

First edition 2019

Printed in the United States of America

www.wingspanpress.com

Library of Congress Control Number 2019934849

1 2 3 4 5 6 7 8 9 10

SUNLIGHT, SHADOWS, AND ECHOES

THIS IS DEDICATED

TO THOSE WHO GAVE ME

ENCOURAGEMENT AND DIRECTION

TO DEVELOP AND PRESENT THESE WRITINGS:

MY WIFE VICKIE

MY BROTHER CHUCK AND HIS WIFE JANE

ALAN BAXTER AND CHESTER JOHNSON

EVIE IVY AND MARVIN FELIX CAMILLO JR.

River of Time

left in solitude

    avoiding a chance

        to awaken

looking back

    at the comedy

        of experience

time rages on

    while we are pulled

        mightily

            through it

like branches and flotsam

    bewildered by

        a river's journey

unaware of any

    destination

David A. Folds

before we know it

. another

month, year, decade

has come

and vanished

and paid us little

for our time

the journal

for our lives

sits on a flat

progression

except for the few

and only occasional

peaks and valleys

but luckily

we do not view it

like this

most of our time

we do find some peace

in this ignorance

3/21/18 - Jersey City, NJ, USA

3

David A. Folds

Jersey Morning

on a hot sunny Sunday

starting with impatient

rays of sun

squeezing sharply between

the slats of our blinds

rising from our bed

I look between

the stretched slats

out to the east

a view of the Hudson

with an early sail floating

white above the blue water

an oasis of peace

between me and a view

of busy buildings

across in Manhattan

-- looking from slower, quiet

out to the complexity of NYC

8/21/2016 - Jersey City, NJ, USA

David A. Folds

The Balconies

Paris flows over you

    like a tide of beauty

      and charm

buildings everywhere

    more than a century old

most with the characteristic balconies

    from the eighteen eighties

in the Latin Quarter

    some are enhanced by

      brilliant red flowers

a few with

    quiet diners

      seated on the third floor

      above the traffic

while the panoramic scenes

up high in the Eiffel

show a wealth

of balconies

in all directions

and the many

irregular shapings

of city blocks

and streets

display a complex

rhythm of the life

in Paris

10/2/16 - Paris, France

David A. Folds

Jazz Piano

my brother Chuck

plays the piano

he really does

when I was a young teen

and he was an older one

he was submerged in jazz

and I swam some with him

Chuck learned to play

before hearing

that music

practicing on classical

and playing

late forties pop

but Basie was a revelation

    --- Jumping at the Woodside

and Chuck was started

    on a long all-encompassing journey

later, now, over sixty years

    he's still a jazz master

as a co-worker

    who once heard him

      said

he plays a lot of piano

hear the complex harmonies

    the melodic beauty

    how he really swings

now hear the stride ---

--- Man

10/12/16 - road to Amsterdam in Germany

David A. Folds

Badminton

when television

    began

        in the States

the networks

    fell in love

        with tennis

one or two cameras

    trying to capture

        images and angles

unsophisticated

        compared to today

and in black and white

meanwhile

    they completely

        forgot about

        badminton

badminton

the most widely played

racquet sport

now

in the world

by the fifties

U.S. could boast

one male

and two female

former singles world champions

all largely unrecognized

David A. Folds

American media

    still ignores

    badminton's global

      popularity

it being easily

    the fastest

    and most taxing

      of all racquet sports

    also the most complex

    and varied

      in shots

      and strategy

time to wake up

    American sports media

3/25/17 - Jersey City, NJ, USA

Sunlight, Shadows, and Echoes

An Odyssey - 1965

he stood half-focused

on twilight's evolving displays

multi-shades –

orange, crimson, yellow

shaping and reshapings

within the escape of the sun

all pointing the way –

to be followed, soon

but now time to return

inside for rest

to prime towards

new beginning

David A. Folds

sweeping changing visions

within a deep slumber

moved in and out of

hints of

reward or harm

subconscious projections

of a possible future

soon to be revealed -

perhaps … perhaps

velvet green

undulating hills

distant blue water

last images floating by

before eyes awoke

the reality of change

        began to emerge

as he gathered

        belongings

two suitcases

        one shoulder bag

from space not stripped

        but missing

                certain key pieces

here remained here

        like an echo

but there not here

        would house

        the new reality

David A. Folds

in the bus depot

    people sat as though

        waiting for a doctor

two women talking - one too loud

a child complaining

and a baby

    wet and tired

        starting to cry – uncaring

teenagers eying food dispensers

    - which candy - what beverage

uninteresting, but do stay awake

    don't drift to sleep

        and miss the call

    for the bus

        is eventually coming

once the sun had set

    motion continued but

    the view out the window

        became more vague

the sound of the motor

    the occasional side force

        rocked him toward sleep

then he was out

    until slowed motion

    and night lights outside

        stirred him and others

    announcing a next stop

one young couple

    stepping down greeted

        by excited family

    parents smiling

        youngsters shouting

David A. Folds

but, just a pit stop for most riders

out briefly – business done

back on board

off into the night

then next morning

stepping off

at another stop

with a four hour wait

with time to stretch

to look around

to eat

in a diner

like so many others

… everywhere

offering a decent

not too expensive

breakfast

waiting

    already with coffee

        for a chosen omelet

while two young girls

    in a booth nearby

    try to flirt

        like grownups

    but obviously

        just like girls

their wishes could be

    his troubles

just look the other way

    ignore

David A. Folds

and after eating

slowly

time to look around

but

being nursemaid

to his luggage

the only good choice

was back to the station

to sit quietly

avoid eye contact

especially with locals

wanting no new problem

no challenges

for almost three hours

now another bus

      another seat

            at a window

but by mid-afternoon

      it became the side

            with the sun

heat rays engulfing

      his area

nothing to do except

      to lower hat

            over brow

and wait it out

passing farmlands

      and train tracks

            occasionally

               near the road

David A. Folds

all this land

    quickly passing by

      is our land

not under its

    own control

except for the rivers

    and the mountains

      both too powerful

        to dominate

and also the wild lands

    left alone by choice

      for our human pleasure

we rule as primary group

    but not as individuals

as just one we are small

    all across the Earth

early evening

    in the middle

        of nowhere

something was wrong

the bus slowed

    slipped to the side

        of the highway

            and stopped cold

the driver explained

    the bus had a problem

        they all had a problem

the solution would be

    a replacement

        not a part

            but an entire bus

David A. Folds

how soon?

       about three hours

   waiting out in the middle

     of nowhere

   with the replacement

      arrived and working

  his destination

      was reached eventually

        late in the night

  too late to find lodging

  he could try to sleep

     in the station

       until closing

 and then outside

     on a bench

      roughly

waiting out there

    to greet

        a new solar beginning

a new stage

    of his life

        on a new platform

finally the sun had

    fully arrived

life was starting

    to stir

        in the town

it was time

    to find another

        breakfast diner

David A. Folds

regain energy

reach a coffee

awakening

prepare to

present himself

for a wished for

hoped for job

locating the place

asking

who he should see

directed to a

middle-aged man

in a gaudy suit

introducing himself

    he saw this man

        shake his head

he said

    you're really late

    besides

        the boss's nephew

           got the position

sorry

    nothing I can do for you

David A. Folds

what next?

    stay and search

    just go back

either one

    presented no answers

gather yourself think

    you must decide

1/23/17-3/717 - Jersey City, NJ, USA

David At 2 1/2

David 2 1/2

> bold and brave

> > like his biblical

> > > namesake

> and family

> > from New Hampshire

> visiting Midwest relatives

<u>first</u>

> in the grandparents' home

> where his father told

> > his own parents

> we do not punish

> > our children

> > > if possible

only use reason

David A. Folds

Grandma found little David

in the living room

standing on

the grand piano

she took a deep breath

and then said

David, you would not

stand on the piano

in your home

would you?

the reply was

we don't have a piano

in our home

<u>second</u>

  some days later

   at the large

    family cottage

     in Wisconsin

a beautiful summer day

  mother sitting

   in the screened

    sitting porch

     knitting

  looking down the hill

  below

   to the pier

David A. Folds

there was David

and when she saw

no one else

her heart rate

went up

watching closely, now

she saw him

lean over

to look at the water

and quickly fall in

of course

she screamed

this pier had one side

for boats

and

the other

for swimming

the side for swimming

was cleared of seaweed

but the other was not

of course

he fell into the side for boats

moving up and down

among the seaweed

up and down

until he

was pulled out

he was ok

but his mother and aunt

were hysterical

he could not

understand

why they were so upset

he was really embarrassed

for them

4/6/17 - Jersey City, NJ, USA

David A. Folds

Transitions

Spring was not so kind

as to stay with us

with gentle weather

leaving us to transit

into the harsh

throbbing heat

air and pavement

baking intensely

in the sunlight

while we look for the shaded

softer side

we think of better moments

away at the beach

or blanketed by

cold AC

wishing to pass through

to descending Autumn

sooner

but neutral Autumn will

lead us into

white frigid snow

again we will have lost

the gentle weather

7/7/17 - Jersey City, NJ, USA

David A. Folds

Mothers

my mother's mother

quietly strong

widowed with two children

survived ... turning her home

into a boarding house

in 1915

soft but firmly

raised my mother to succeed

to go on to Smith College

and then to Yale for a Masters

my mother, her daughter

started a career

but surrendered it

to marry, support her husband

and raise us

... two demanding brothers

like her mother

    she was soft

    quiet in the background

        always loving, caring

personal wishes

    rarely to be primary

she lived first

    for her three males

        who were not always

            so soft as she

for many years

    she supported her husband's work

        who was in the same field

        as her Masters

he described her assistance

    as invaluable

done with no

    aboveboard recognition

David A. Folds

much later after

I had wandered though

significant years

always with her support

and that of my father

she quickly bonded

with my wife to be

bringing me delight to

see their strong friendship

after the first 17 years

after her husband stopped working

they moved to

a retirement community

where she too

could feel retired

she was then 86

for 11 more years

she lived with

developing memory issues

supported more and more

by my dad, her husband

as needed

a retired friend

a doctor

seeing how much effort

Dad devoted to this care

(he, himself, almost as elderly)

said: "Tom, I don't know how you do it"

the reply was: "I owe it to her"

she passed quietly at 97

7/11/17 - Jersey City, NJ, USA

David A. Folds

Life Underneath

beneath the asphalt

and the cement

life exists

in the soil

amidst the rock bed

above the tunnels

of the trains

and the tunnels for

water and electric

and for the modern wires

that link you to me

life exists

that knows nothing

of man's marvels

that simply tries

to exist

and progress

from moment to moment

doing this more simply

than you or me

8/31/17 - Jersey City, NJ, USA

David A. Folds

Perspectives

across the vast

     horizons of our dreams

exist

     large flatlands

     dramatic peaks

     verdant valleys

     dominant waters

     and

     spreading wastelands

a mixed salad

     of true experience

our hopes strain

to escape

the flat repetition

we panic from vertigo

on our highest climbs

and waste away

the beauty

of the peaceful land

fearing the force

of the ocean storms

wondering

what became

of all our dreams

9/28/17 - Jersey City, NJ, USA

David A. Folds

Tales of My Father

tales have been told

from when humans

began to talk

sometimes embellishing

reality

or to falsify

or establish myths

but my father's tales

are not like those

for all the years I shared

life with him

I never knew of

anything he said

that was ever

untrue within his understanding

he never feared

the truth

and it was always

sufficient

and complete

that is how life should be

David A. Folds

1.

surely the young flow

aggressively

from hot to cold

from wise to

carelessly stupid

such that

there he was

punishment

for misbehaving

standing

in the classroom corner

when the Principal

burst in, asking

for him by name

it seems he had won

a state-wide student

essay contest

on Lincoln

the teacher pointed

to red-faced Tom

in the corner

at the time

he was more embarrassed

than proud

only to be amused

much later

retelling to his sons

David A. Folds

2.

creativity flowing

    at a young age

with a friend

    and a small

        early twentieth century

        printing machine

they published a weekly

    neighborhood newspaper

gathering items

    focused both on the young

    and on adults

he drawing any illustrations

    as co-editor

    and writer

3.

much later

    entering college

journalism

    was the target

and in his freshman year

    at Yale

on assignment

    for the newspaper

he was sent to see

    a man planning

to be the first to fly

    across the wide Atlantic

David A. Folds

his visit was late

after all had left

except Lindbergh

this soon to be

aviation giant

treated him with respect

answering all his questions

even letting him be

the last to sit

in the cockpit

before the next

morning's historic flight

but, my father is not even

a small asterisk

to this history

except for a few

of us

<u>4.</u>

fortune does smile

    at unexpected

        moments, sometimes

after two more college years

    the summer before

        the Stock Market crash

there was a chance

    to see Europe

        with his brother

accompanying a wealthy

    maiden aunt

David A. Folds

his mind and soul

were captivated

by art

at the highest level

they almost had to

drag him out of

all the great museums

seeing the originals

was much more intense

than pictures in books

after this

journalism

had faded

to be a painter

an artist

was the new ambition

5.

at one point

        fortune smiles

then turns its back

        at another

with a new

        exciting ambition

the results of

        the crash of '29

meant that

        his family

        could not support him

        for a

        second degree

David A. Folds

he would have to fund

his continued art schooling

somehow

himself

he tried selling

shoes door to door

too honest to promote

poor quality products

he failed

at that

he conceived ideas

for joke cartoons

illustrating

and selling them

to humor publications

and selling some of the ideas

to famous cartoonists

and using more time and energy

he washed dishes

in an Italian eatery

but one night was so hot

the washers stripped

off all their clothes

down to just their aprons

only to have the manager

rush in saying

the owner and wife

would step back there

shortly

the only fast solution was

to turn the aprons around

wearing shorts

could be assumed

David A. Folds

6.

marriage changes things

some change is obvious

some more subtle

married in the middle

of the Great Depression

meant that

the idea of

the starving artist

would really starve

and with two mouths

to feed

even worse

and again fortune

smiled for him

Exeter education

included no Art

he had degrees

    in English and Art

and was brought in

    to the English Department

        to gradually start one for Art

he dove into it

    aggressively

        eventually being

            a one man band

teaching Art

    appreciation, history,

    sketching, painting,

    sculpture, photography,

    and scene design

his own painting

    lost out

his art had become his teaching

David A. Folds

7.

by 1940

    he was a father twice

        I came second

and parenting lead him

    to consider creating

        a children's book

it was based on a real

    childhood experience

an exciting nighttime

    fire alarm

he brought my brother and me

    to the local firehouse

he sketched uniforms

    equipment

        fire engines

and his two excited sons

were thrilled

the result was

a successful publication

"Where is the Fire"

written and drawn

by my father

but this was not

a new vocation

only a one-time excursion

David A. Folds

8.

when war broke out

he looked to enlist

but he was over thirty

married

twice a father

and an educator

he passed the physicals easily

including showing

his ability to

walk on his hands

they asked if he had

coached teams

the answer was

scene design for theater

not enough for Officer material

the military saw more value

for him to remain civilian

9.

after the war

    his work at Exeter

        led to a college offer

Northwestern would bring

    him in as

        Art Department Chairman

he, himself,

    would teach

        Art history and

            appreciation

    for which he had no degree

but, he proved to be a

    masterful teacher

        way above average

David A. Folds

he also upgraded

the entire department

including the

slide library

at that time

slide projection

was basic

to Art education

he created many new slides

including special

close-ups

showing important details

one summer

still in high school

I handled the projector

I saw how creative

he had become

in the classroom

10.

the first educational

      broadcast on Art

           for color TV

was delivered by him

      in Chicago

we all watched

      behind a glass window

as usual

      his talk was

           clear

                brilliant

asking Granddad if he was proud

      he said:

           "Of course, he's my first-born"

David A. Folds

11.

while in Evanston

    The Art Institute commissioned him

        to travel to New York

            to arrange for a

                one-man exhibit

Kitty his wife would come, too

it was for a soon to be rising artist

    living in the Lower Eastside

        William de Kooning

he had finished works

    but none had titles

many years later

    going to the Whitney

        with my father

entering the first room

    for a retrospective on de Kooning

stopping at the first painting

    he said: "Your mother named that"

and among the early paintings

    all were named

        by one or the other

           or both

but only de Kooning

    and they two

        knew that

David A. Folds

12.

while at Northwestern

and also later

as a consultant for

various corporations

he advised them on purchases

of art that would

have more value and prestige

later

they were proudly displaying them

at corporate headquarters

he enriched the corporations

but had no resources

to invest for himself

we would never know

how much

his income

could have grown

13.

to our surprise

  Ford asked him to make

    a series of commercials

      for the new Ford model

commercials then were

  more sedate

    less impactful

      than those we see now

it was like walking a tight-rope

  for him

    to satisfy them

  and still maintain

    his academic

      integrity

David A. Folds

he never really praised

the Ford

but related various things in Art

to the shape and looks

of the car

the adds were broadcast

during the very popular

Ford Theater

on Sunday nights

for many weeks

in 1957

he bought a new Chevy

10/24/17 - Jersey City, NJ, USA

The Light That Owns Us

the Sun

further than anything

beyond what our

mathematical calculations

can comprehend

holds us in its

almost infinite arms

like a long-distant

parent

but, too close

and we perish

too far

and we freeze

David A. Folds

when our section

of Earth's globe

hides from the rays

most of the sub rosa

of our lives occur

the bright heat

of what we call day

stirs the intensity

of activity

and looks to spotlight

the moments of truth

and the moments

when truth fails

as the clouds shift

and move along

we look upward

and say

"Oh, it's the Sun"

5/28/18 - Jersey City, NJ, USA

David A. Folds

Early in Connecticut

when we were in

the spring bud

of our time

we traveled north

to a colder

clime

in the late autumn

Connecticut

morning

on a family visit

the first for you

to begin to build

on relationships for

our lasting future

you were not exactly well

would have wished to refuse

but for my insisting

your Saints supporting

trying your best

you proved your heart

true quality

shone through

11/4/17 - Jersey City, NJ, USA

David A. Folds

Time and Motion

left in solitude

    avoiding a chance

        to awaken

to turn within

we seek to invent

    reality

imagine activity

    ignoring stillness

static objects

    sway or dance

the spot on the

wall crawls

like some insect

the power of

our weakness

still defeats

once again

a formless softer time

3/--/17 completed 11/29/17 - Jersey City, NJ, USA

David A. Folds

Filters

while the wind

    will shift things

        any way it wants

we still seek to perceive

    what our rigid minds

        have already mapped out

awake

    everything that reaches

    our senses

is accepted or not

    but always filtered

    our inner constructs

        will not want to feed on

    raw data

asleep

    our sub consciousness

      can flow through

endless connected or separate

    images and instances

filtered or not

    like a journey through

      an endless

        meandering cavern

but passing through

    in free-flowing dreams

then

    when awake again

      we forget most of it

4/16/18 - Jersey City, NJ, USA

David A. Folds

From Mom and Dad

born in the frantic surge

of industrial expanse

raised in the righteousness

of a war to end all wars

growing to reach adulthood

while the twenties roared

they found each other

we ... my brother and I

emerged in the purity

of their world

trying to find

our own sense of purity

we climbed or stumbled

our vines seeking light

supported by their

constant care and concern

somehow we found

along with their help

our own true

paths of peace

4/25/18 - Jersey City, NJ, USA

David A. Folds

Wind in the Trees

a soft wind

    brushed by my ear

bushes dancing

    at their own level

branches and their leaves

    floating while

      they splay

        this way and that

but the trees with thick

    midsections and

      solid covered bark

        resist this gentle wind

walking forward

    we slice through

        the lesser

            impacts of nature

our lives grasping them only

      at our peripheral awareness

we travel mostly

     hermetically sealed

        through time and space

while a soft wind

     brushes by our ear

5/7/18 - Jersey City, NJ, USA

David A. Folds

Energy

the hovering

    of a hummingbird

the walking waddle

    of a pigeon

a dolphin's dance

    over blue waters

all display the rich

    curving spiral

    evident

      around us

we breath in

    absorbing myriad

      microorganisms

and then

    when deflating

      oust most of them

the wonder is that

we can even consider

how much of

existence

there is

that quickly

passes us by

6/17/18 - Jersey City, NJ, USA

David A. Folds

The Speed of Life

while the world

mostly sleeps

change continues

but at a speed

like shifting of

tectonic plates

or the expanse

or contraction

of a glacier

we take every

slow step

towards

more of the same

we reach milestones

    that are like

        what came before

            likely what will follow

we wake up to

    each new day

        expecting

            more of the same

but hoping for something

    to be different

7/3/18 - Jersey City, NJ, USA

David A. Folds

Earthly Struggles

while windmills warp daliesque

the flowing current is

influenced into

irregular ellipses

and reason stumbles

like an overloaded sot

now we can forget

briefly

the constant battle

to maintain our balance

in this volatile uncaring

earthbound wisdom

wrapped in constant change

a constantly demanding

form of flesh

feeding what our

desires cry for

forgetting what

our soul

our higher inner

spirit waits for

while we remain

sadly wrapped within

this lower world

8/16/18 - Jersey City, NJ, USA

David A. Folds

Dusk

by the water

peaceful and serene

early evening's gradually

dimming light

catches the crest

of ripples

flowing west

to shore

as if to escape

the intensity

from the east

of many still

brightly lit lights

of Manhattan

we have walked into the calm

of the quiet

of a slower

rhythm

without thinking

our breath

quiets

our pulse rate

slows down

embracing our

panoramic

dreamscape

8/23/18 - Jersey City, NJ, USA

David A. Folds

Toledo - Old and New

above and across

from Toledo

ancient but now

in our presence

on the same hill

that great El Greco

viewed and painted

the panoramic

beauty emanating

from the Toledo

of his day

we pause

to breathe in

mentally and spiritually

all the magnificence

before rushing

to focus and frame

our cameras

trying to capture

a small bit

of this wonder

9/14/18 - Torremolinos, Spain

David A. Folds

True Freedom

my soul

    entrapped

        in earthly body

sleepwalks

    through much of life

my sensory impact

    and thought games

      still dominate

        awareness

hoping for at least

    a middle level

    calm

but often focused

    on life success

where and when

can I open

the essence

of higher spirit

how can I let

my imprisoned soul

fly free

to dance

in the

vastness

of eternity

9/24/18 - Jersey City, NJ, USA

David A. Folds

Barriers

through the mist

    veiled rays of light

        invade the mostly shaded

    mostly quiet

        realm of dawn

the soft pulse

    of morning

      just beginning

awaits the full

    thrust of the force

      of brightness

trees, flowers and other plants

tilt

slightly to east

assuming already their usual

breakfast baths

of light

we stir

still in morning stupor

stumbling to our usual

bathroom rituals

oblivious to

all the morning's magic

outside the shield

of our protective walls

10/22/18 - Jersey City, NJ, USA

David A. Folds

Paintings in Time

memories float

in and out

of recognition

weaving a pattern

a collage

in our consciousness

with the external

not holding us

entirely captive

past moments and connections

intrude

overlapping the present

the flow of time

    continues relentlessly

while we swim through it

    pulled this way and that

by different memories

    dancing their own way

    in and around

      our prosaic present

10/27/18 - Jersey City, NJ, USA

David A. Folds

Worries and Wishes

the old men

    of the old times

conservatively spoke about

    the destruction

    of change

    the lack of unity

    between established

    and new

while these two collided

    trying to unite

but out of rhythm

    disrupting

    the peace

much later

    conservative

        politicos

posing as saviors

    of all humanity

trying to hold government

    small

        and under their thumbs

David A. Folds

while keeping

business huge

and citizens small

convince voters

they are best

as barely pawns

not even players

and that industry

deserves all the riches

which the small

never share

people ---

be careful

for what you wish

10/17/18 - Jersey City, NJ, USA

Slaughterhouses of America

and eleven dead

in Pittsburgh

death is in the history

of all humans

but inhuman beings

warped visions

interrupt the natural

flow of life

we all will die eventually

but who has the right

to choose when

for others

David A. Folds

the twisted minds of cowards

look to attack

in the sanctuaries

the churches, the temples,

the schools

places of peace and safety

never where police

or the military abide

the hell in the killer's

heart and mind

is well deserved

but victims and families

drown in a punishment

of innocence

while the pattern

    of this violence

        floods the media

which profits

    and tells this story

        to twisted copycats

so that no peace

    will be

        with us

11/1/18 - Jersey City, NJ, USA

David A. Folds

Questions

where to begin?

--- here?

if not now

then when?

the sun

braver than us

rises towards its glory

with no hesitation

no remorse

while we

stunned from sleep

seek to postpone

our rising

still half lost

in the echoes

of our elusive

floating dreams

we breathe in

    only in the moment

surrounded by our bit

    of the earthly world

focused on just what's

    before our noses

but are we mortal?

    certainly our bodies

are we immortal?

    possibly our spirits

if both are so

    why is it so hard

    to choose

      what's important?

David A. Folds

with the body

only a temporary

vessel

on part of a journey

going beyond its boarders

sail inside

as smooth as you can

but spend some time

looking far beyond

the scope

of your horizon

11/4/18 - Jersey City, NJ, USA

Sunlight, Shadows, and Echoes

Realm of the Wind

the wind washes over

and sometimes

through us

amorphic in the essence

of instability

not actually a thing

as we think of such

but really a force

moving, changing

every instant

everywhere

David A. Folds

change is not just coming

change is always

even if ever

so slight

we feel the wind

pushing, moving

our atmosphere

like a river of air

while we try to float

and survive

within it

our full world

    is like one atom

to the totality of

    existence

but we continue

    and sometimes flourish

moving onward

    spurred by the

insistence of

    our central

    nervous system

the internal wind

    that moves us

12/5/18 - Jersey City, NJ, USA

David A. Folds

The Kiss

the touch of your lips

reaches past the sensory

sometimes electric moment

reestablishing recementing

the meaning

of our experience

declaring as much

as the simple

but for some difficult

I love you

spoken everyday between us

solid as granite

telling the story

of synaptic

union between

two spirits

long in touch

long together

12/25/18 - Jersey City, NJ, USA

111   David A. Folds

Blue

the color is blue

and the morning

is coming

deep dark blue

in transition

softening

clearing

reaching toward

the brilliant clarity

of a royal blue

more perfect than

we deserve

our minds floating

above in the eternity

of the thought

of the realm of

skies of blue

our rhythms absorbing

the lapping waves

in the repetition of

water aqua blue

David A. Folds

our hopes

some of the time

will reach for the peace

in the softness

of a powder blue

but we end our day with

noncommittal

blue gray shades

and we're still stuck

in neutral

any worse and

we'll have

the blues

12/24/18 - Jersey City, NJ, USA

David A. Folds

Index of Poems by Titles

David A. Folds

www.ingramcontent.com/pod-product-compliance
Lightning Source LLC
La Vergne TN
LVHW011401080426
835511LV00005B/379